For Sage,
my partner on the journey,
and Norrie and Lucas,
who help light the way

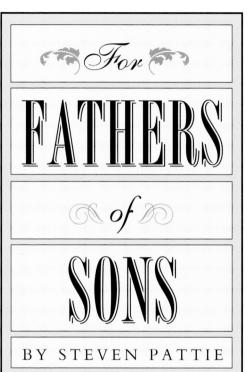

For
FATHERS
of
SONS

BY STEVEN PATTIE

Illustrated by Johnny & Jamie Yates

The C.R. Gibson Company,
Norwalk, Connecticut 06856 U.S.A.

Published by The C.R. Gibson Company, Norwalk, Connecticut 06856
U.S.A.

Johnny Yates, age 9, illustrated the pictures on pages 14, 17, 21 39, 41,
and 43.
Jamie Yates, age 7, illustrated the pictures on pages 27 and 35.

Designed by Deborah Michel
ISBN 0-8378-8828-X
GB513
Made in U.S.A.

INTRODUCTION

◁═◦◦◦═▷

In the Old Testament is the story of how the nation of Israel miraculously crosses the Jordan River. In order to serve as a sign among God's people and to preserve the memory of such an extraordinary event, a monument of stones is built at the river's edge. It is said that the reason for the assembled rocks is that when the children ask, "What do these stones mean?"

the story will be told and remembered. "These stones," declares Joshua, "are to be a memorial to the people of Israel forever (Joshua 4:15-24)."

❧

And so, to the present day, the people of Israel have not forgotten.

❧

Since the day I made my crossing into the territory of fatherhood, I've become keenly aware of how precious, yet transitory, these early years are. One moment, my sons were born. The next, we were celebrating their first birthdays at the nearby park in the coolness of an October afternoon. In the blink of an eye, I was posing with them for pictures of their first day of kindergarten a few Septembers later. The words from Ecclesiastes about the sun rising and the sun going down, and hastening to the place where it rises, were thoughts my heart understood.

~~~~~~~

As a young father, everything about my boys continually amazed me—what they saw and how they described it, the joys and concerns they expressed, and so much more. Amidst the often routine regimen of daily living I found myself frequently awakened by their fresh and insightful vantage points regarding God, themselves, others and their world. I recall the feelings of loss when leaving for work in the morning, the thoughts and observations of two little boys I would miss while on the job.

~~~~~~~

I did not want to miss out on those events that brought tears to their eyes, nor those moments of awe and amazement, magical things for a child, like the coming and going of the Tooth Fairy. Their world of childhood is a magical time filled with a brightness of being that will be largely unparalleled at any other point in their life.

◇◆◇

And so I began to write and to memorialize these wonderful moments, so that our own poetic edifice could be built, and these things could be told and remembered by our family and the generations who follow.

◇◆◇

This small monument of words and remembrances is what this collection of poetry is all about. These are souvenirs of the most wonderful kind.

◇◆◇

My hope is that fathers and grandfathers who read this work will share a few of my own family's moments and be encouraged in their own personal memories and current experience. When our children and grandchildren look back upon their lives and ask, "What did all this mean?" my hope for all of us is that there will be a ready testament through the stones we have gathered, oral and written remembrances for us, for them, and for future generations to enjoy.

STEVEN PATTIE

Sons are a heritage from the Lord,
children are a reward from Him.
Like arrows in the hands of a warrior
are sons born in one's youth.
Blessed is the man
whose quiver is full of them.

PSALMS 127:3-5A

PSALM FOR YOUNG FATHERS

Lord,
we are told
not to weary in doing good.

I am weary again tonight
and I confess it again
with my lips.

My actions confess my weariness.
In my hesitation to read the last familiar story
read so many times before.
In my anxious yearnings for a deep breath, space,
and time,
and believing I need more.

I am weary again tonight.
There is no more to be given
from this good and loving heart.
Feeling as an old tree heavily laden
with these light young blossoms and green fruit
I seem so slowly to be uprooted
from the earth.

Assure me again,
Remind us,
an exercised heart is a better fruit.
Remind us,
the untested heart a bitter one.

Assure me,
and sustain us,
that these limbs not break
as we carry unto ripeness
tomorrow's sweet produce
and maturity
in doing good.

Loud Tears

Loud tears
of a midnight child
fills a late, dark, middle-night's hour.

He and I let them fall,
and I catch them,
in praying hands cupped to receive.

❧

One-Piece Pajamas

Wearing his purple one-piece pajamas
he crawls in a marching sort of way,
looking like an overripe plum.

Sweet.

At Bedtime

At bedtime,
high-pitched voices matched and assigned
to trolls and teddy bears,
sufficient friends for the day,
hush to a quiet as darkness falls.
The temperature
of their plastic bodies and friendly faces
warmed by hands by day
are cold and still in their aloneness by night
this evening.

At bedtime,
their host leaves them in a queue
along the floor
on his way to bed,
no two alike.
Everyone and everything quiet now.

At bedtime,
the spell is broken
by the good-nights and I love yous not uttered.
The quiet is so quiet,
for each is on his way to bed.
Fantasy failing for longer moments,
the monologue of dialogue long asleep.

QUIET QUAKING

You're beginning to imagine
the terror
of finally speaking sentences
that will be public and understood by too many,
leaving too soon and too soon forgotten
a language of sweet words and gesticulese.

I saw you one night,
sitting up erect on the edge of your bed,
long after you had been put there
and just a few minutes before my own rest.
Sitting and wondering,
I sensed a quiet quaking
about the rumors of things to come.

Too often has the evening damp
co-mingled with your tears.
I don't know what they mean
but only that my presence next to yours
quiets and settles your soft spirit.

Doing It Like Daddy

I had thought he was content,
puttering alongside of mom
at knee level,
punkering with pans from the cupboard.

But then his gaze caught mine from the little room
where he sleeps and clothes are laundered.
Suddenly his contentment evaporated
and he came running with eyes laughing
to the march of feet surer by day.
He breaks into a run,
he looks into my eyes.
I move the newspaper aside
as he mutters and hums his love.

He then clambers from me onto the couch,
closely settled next to me,
his back against the sofa.
Grabbing a piece of the newspaper
he positions himself
and reads like his daddy,
looking to make sure he's doing it just right.

YOU ALWAYS SEE ME OFF

You always see me off to work
from a place of your appointment,
logically and usually the front door,
or the gate by the front of the house.

At the moment you sense I'm on my way,
you stop whatever you're doing,
a ceasing without regret.

You hug me,
and then we kiss each other lightly.
Yours is always concluded with a little smack,
and then quickly punctuated with a "bye,"
and the wave of your right hand.

And then I'm off, and down the path,
while you return to carry on with your day.

It Is Always Your Two Feet

It is always your two feet I hear first,
one dropping quickly after the other,
with some carefulness
and carelessness to the floor.

With your determined little gait you march in.
I always see the small top portion of your head first,
as you come my way.
I look forward to the rest of you,
as you walk round to my side of the bed,
where with your two middle fingers
secure in your mouth
you begin jumping with some impatience,
and to the accompaniment of desire,
for me to bring you to myself.
I grab you underneath the arms,
and pull you to my chest,
where you love to be my little daddy's boy.

You are never still for long,
and your nails on rhythmic fingers
alarm my neck this morning.

I react with pain and you laugh,
you always think it's funny,
and that's the way it usually goes.
You wonder when I'll open my eyes,
for you already know that lids are made for opening.
Eventually our eyes couplet
and we laugh some more.
Sillier and sillier we become,
amused at nothing in particular but one another.
When you start your jumping and falling,
my head still buried in a pillow
I call for a truce,
and suggest it is time to go to the bathroom
to carry on with the day.

You slide out
and I follow you
to the bathroom.
You drag the stool
out from behind the toilet
and put it next to the sink
where you watch me shave
with amazement and amusement.
The lime lather is on my face,

and you always want
a little spot of it on your hand,
never your cheek.
While I shave
you wash off the bit at the tip
of your finger
in what you call
some baby water
from the tap,
the amount is so small.
I rinse my face,
you rinse yours,
I grab my towel,
and you grab your brother's,
and together we dry our faces,
ready for the day.

TENDING HIS GARDEN

He is lord,
tending his garden
and exercising dominion.
The organizer now
of his chaotic little world.

The little cars and containers,
this odd and that end,
are put into boxes and things.
And then, removing and trying
again and again,
for simply the joy it brings.

THE QUESTION

I asked him as we at the pictures looked,
and petted the backs
of the funny ones,
if he was as one of them.

Are you a caterpillar,
like he on the leaf of the tree?
And he shook his head and said his long-drawn, "No,"
My son was not at all like he.

Then are you as the turtle,
swimming there in the sea?
And he shook his head and said his long-drawn, "No,"
My son was not at all like he.

Would you then possibly be a bear,
like him taking honey from the bee?
And he shook his head and said his long-drawn, "No,"
My son was not at all like he.

And so I asked him the obvious question now,
Are you a little boy I see?
And he shook his head and said his long-drawn, "No,"
"A man," said he,
pointing to me.

Playing with the Plug

He poked fun at the idea
of an untimely leaving from this world.
Playing with the plug,
the instinctive drama was introduced.

Stop me Daddy,
I'm a baby playing with a plug,
and you don't want me to get a bad shock.

And so I was tested,
and my commitment to his life.

Tooth Fairy

When I wake,
brightly up in the morning,
the tooth will be gone,
and the fairy too.

But in the little pocket
of this special tooth pillow
will be a small treat.

The Tooth Fairy will come through the door
and put the prize in.
She will come this very night with her lots of treats
and carrying a bag of pennies.
Whatever you want you can wish.
Aren't you glad we can wish whatever we want?

This little pocket
is made only of thread,
but it will guard the tooth.
Isn't that amazing?

I will make a wish now,
for a penny or candy.
I can't tell you what the wish is,
or else the fairy won't come.

The Tooth Fairy will come this very night.
I'll try to get candies for you and me.
She must have amazing powers.
She must have amazing powers.

GIFTS ESPECIALLY FOR ME

He brought gifts this evening
made especially for me.

Yesterday I helped him make a Valentine,
a piece of red paper decorated with a white doily
and a scattering of glitter—
never a clue that it was for me.

Today I helped him build a castle,
a rolled up piece of blue paper,
glued upright upon a goldenrod plane—
never a clue that it was for me.

Tonight, so excited about his surprise,
he brought these gifts,
made especially for me.

Yesterday

Yesterday,
you were busy playing with all these.
Today, they remain where you left them.
Gone for a few days with your mom,
they're parked like you'll be back
with the next breeze.

The trucks and the tractors
are in their familiar line-up.
Truck beds and shovels
filled with dirt and rocks and bits of tree trash,
are hard at play in imaginary work,
just where you left them
yesterday.

Wonderful Notion

No one come near this hole
and not dig
or take away
my seed
cause I want a tree.
If anybody takes this seed
you go to jail.

That a large waxen-leafed
magnolia,
could spring from the small
crimson seed,
was amazing to him.

An awesome thought
for a four-year-old to take in,
the wonderful notion of something so important
in such a small package.

A little seed.
Carried home carefully from school,
wrapped in a soft white napkin
tightly pinched between his two fingers.

He voiced concern
that there were so many trees already in his yard.
But starting so little
he seemed sure it would
make it's own place
in this world.

He found a place for its planting
in the dry bed of his sandbox.
Sterile except for minerals left by old rainfall,
and some indiscriminate fertilizing by cats.
A barren place amidst apparent impossibilities
like the tales of the Bible,
like some stories of today.

Notes On a
Little Child's Sadness

Sadness reigns when seeds don't grow
in a sandbox bed, he didn't know.

When his caterpillar is eaten by a hungry bird
he cannot understand why a friend is preferred.

A rude rain never turning to snow
leaves a desert boy sad for what he will never know.

Birds chirping for a mother long flown
tears his eyes, by themselves now alone.

The binding broken on a favorite book
makes him sorry for the care forsook.

Leaves falling from the nameless tree
upsets instincts, he can collect but three.

A poor man wracked with hunger and thirst
leaves him wondering how the last will be first.

His hamster dead by an accidental squeeze
makes him think again about the power to seize.

Hearing a child filleted by an insensitive dad
feeds his passion to save the glad heart of the sad.

Saying goodbye to laughing friends today
he remembers the love, the words he wanted to say.

Taking care of his sad little brother
makes him glad he shares his toys with no other.

Leg Songs

It was hard for him to imagine
something singing without its mouth,
but I had said it did,
and he believed.

Together we listened to the cricket
that sang with his legs,
in the close but dark distance.

It sounded strange to him,
and now it sounded strange to me,
an adult too familiar
with the strange and the silly,
until led by a child
to places I remember.

Patience and Pretending

He is already reminiscing
about the days of his babyhood.
Pretending, we changed his diapers again
and laughed together,
assured that I still have the patience
to do as I once did.

The Tree House

I had one like it once.
It was faraway in the corner of the yard,
where things were mysterious,
but where I was always within earshot
of calling for my dad, just in case.

This is their place.
A wild, wonderful tree,
with a discarded table top
set squarely in the branches,
a lookout station for two small boys.

It is very high up,
at least four feet off the ground,
and with many secret ways to get there.
There is even another platform
a few feet higher,
where enemies can be seen coming from afar.

This special place,
faraway in the corner of the yard,
is camouflaged with sticks and leaves and grass,
both boys very sure that these precautions
will keep the intruder away
from this place of their own,
faraway in the corner of the yard.

GOING THE DISTANCE

Nothing could stop you this morning
as you climbed aboard the old two-wheeler
and began your hour of attempts
to master the riding you've reported
your friends are already doing.

Mounted, I gave you easy pushes.
We celebrated your riding and were amazed
at the distances you are already
beginning to travel.

But this learning was just between you and me.
There were boys watching us from a distance,
and I knew that you had noticed them too.

You decided it was time for a rest.
We retreated to the garage,
as you secretly whispered something about
the watching guys.

We will wait together
and talk about how good you've become,
and then return to the road
to practice going the distance.

EASY BYES

It was always
never easy.
The good-byes,
his, "I miss you and I love you,"
his words,
always his words,
were never sufficient,
nor one last hug.

It sometimes made my leaving
so hard,
and often my arriving at work
so late,
and sometimes I wished the leaving easier,
until today.

When so easily he left for school,
hardly saying good-bye.
Young yet already off on his own,
so quickly, so easy
does the leaving become.

No Help Needed

The hard work was over
of raking leaves
and trimming trees.
He'd dragged the sack of garbage by himself today.
No help needed he told me,
and he was right.

We cut and then we clipped
plants and palms and trees.
Back and forth
between me and him
until the cans were full,
in mute testimony to our labor.

And we were very sure
we had worked together very hard.

PROTECTED BY MY JOYING,
IN THE MEMORY
OF THE MORNING

Towards the middle of the day
you came by my office for a visit.
Mommy left you for lunch with me.
Eating and laughing, we talked
about things of interest to you
and now of interest to me.
I wrestled close to your body for a kiss
and away it was brushed
without comment from yourself,
while protected by my joying
in the memory of the morning.

As I tucked you in at the end of the day
in pajamas already two sizes too small,
I forgot for a moment the instruction
that kisses are no longer.
All it took was a wipe of the forearm
and my kiss was removed
from your forehead,
while protected by my joying
in the memory of the morning.

ALREADY DOES HE SPEAK

Already does he speak
of days as a baby,
for him a past long ago.
Dad, do you remember when? questions
punctuate our conversations.

Seeing his brother's bottle lying about
reminds us of what we remember together,
and that while we're together
in the middle somewhere,
we have no end
as father and son.

Wondering if as an adult
I'll be with him as I am today,
I calm his fears, and mine,
assuring us I'll be there,
as from the beginning
until the end.

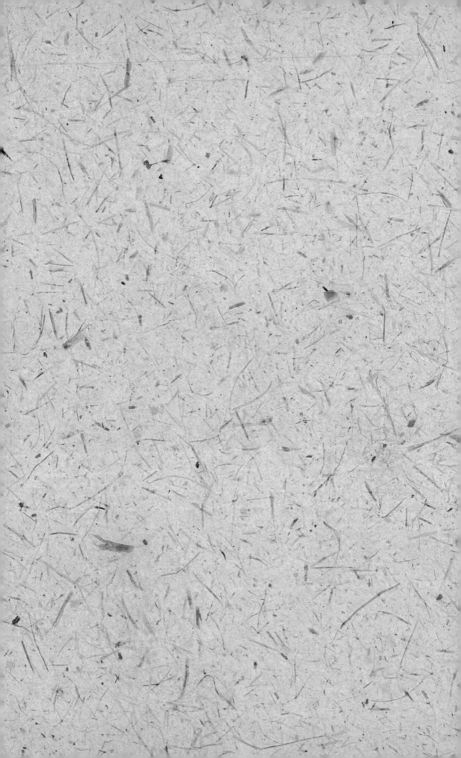